FACT-O-PEDIA

FISH AND AMPHIBIANS

MOONSTONE

Published in Moonstone
by Rupa Publications India Pvt. Ltd 2023
7/16, Ansari Road, Daryaganj
New Delhi 110002

Sales centres:
Prayagraj Bengaluru Chennai
Hyderabad Jaipur Kathmandu
Kolkata Mumbai

Copyright © Rupa Publications India Pvt. Ltd 2023

All rights reserved.
No part of this publication may be reproduced, transmitted,
or stored in a retrieval system, in any form or by any means,
electronic, mechanical, photocopying, recording or otherwise,
without the prior permission of the publisher.

P-ISBN: 978-93-5702-293-4
E-ISBN: 978-93-5702-278-1

First impression 2023

10 9 8 7 6 5 4 3 2 1

This book is sold subject to the condition that it shall not,
by way of trade or otherwise, be lent, resold, hired out, or otherwise
circulated, without the publisher's prior consent, in any form of binding
or cover other than that in which it is published.

Contents

Introduction	6
Rise of Fish	8
Early Jawless and Jawed Fish	10
Osteichthyes	12
Anatomy of Fish - I	14
Anatomy of Fish - II	16
Sharks	18
Predatory Sharks	20
Rays and Skates	22
Venomous Fish	24
Unusual Fish	26
Aquarium Fish	28
Coral Reef Fish	30
Camouflage Fish	32
Balloon Fish	34
Small Sea Predators	36
Fast Swimming Fish	38
Schooling Fish	40
Strange Looking Fish	42
Glossary	44
Answers	46
Introduction	48
Features	50
Evolution	52

Classification	54
Skin	56
Respiration	58
Food Habits	60
Survival Skills	62
Frogs: Characteristics	64
Metamorphosis	66
Frogs Habitats	68
Poisonous Frogs and Toads	70
The World of Toads	72
Salamanders and Newts	74
Unique Salamanders	76
Super Salamanders	78
Caecilians	80
Axolotls	82
Endangered Amphibians	84
Glossary	86
Answers	88

Introduction

Fish are one the most fascinating creatures on the planet Earth. They were also the first vertebrates to evolve. There are more than 30,000 kinds of fish living in the world's oceans, rivers, and lakes. Fish come in all shapes and sizes. Gobies are only 10 cm long, whereas whale sharks are more than 18 m long.

Fish are one of the most colourful sea animals. They have all the colours of the rainbow from bright yellow, blue, green, red and pink to blue, orange, purple and black.

Their rich colours form striking lace-like designs and patterns of stripes and dots. A queen angelfish's yellow and blue colour is a visual delight. Fish have different behaviours and characteristics. Some fish like eels look like snakes and others like puffer fish can puff themselves up like balloons. Some fish are fast swimmers, and some remain buried throughout their lives on the ocean floor.

Rise of Fish

Fish appeared in the Cambrian Period about 510 million years ago. During the Cambrian Period, many major groups of animals appeared. The fossil records of this period demonstrate that during this time, many organisms diversified and evolved.

Ostracoderms

The first fish were called ostracoderms. They were jawless with poorly formed fins. They were also poor swimmers and used to live near the bottom of the ocean. Ostracoderms were covered with a thick bony armour of plates and scales from head to tail.

The *Pteraspis* was a jawless fish. True or False?

Evolution

Fish evolved remarkably during the Silurian Period about 420 million years ago. This period saw a massive growth in the number of different kinds of fish. Jawless fish like the *Pteraspis* prospered, and the first jawed fish appeared. Acanthodians or spiny sharks were the first true jawed fish. They were not too big in size but evolved to become the top predators in the near future.

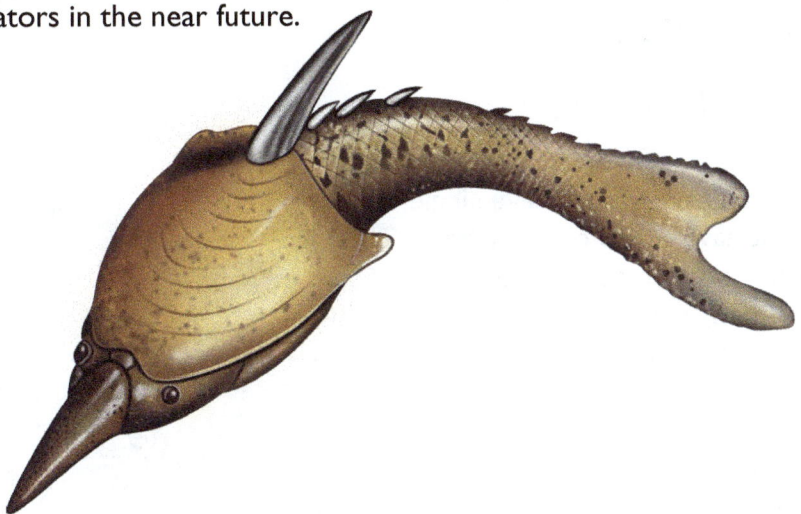

Age of Fishes

Fish flourished during the Devonian Period and were in great abundance. This period is also known as the Age of Fishes. This age witnessed a great rise in placoderms, jawed fish with bony armours, bony fish with a cartilaginous skeleton known as chondrichthians, and fish with a bony skeleton known as Osteichthyes.

Facts

- The Pteraspis has strange, wing-like structures protruding from the back of its gills. It is believed that these wings probably helped it to swim faster.
- The word ostracoderm stands for 'shell-skin'.

Early Jawless and Jawed Fish

The earliest jawless and jawed fish prospered during the Age of Fishes and dominated Earth. The jawed fish placoderms and chondrichthians ruled the oceans and seas. Hagfish and lampreys are the only primitive jawless fish that have withstood various mass extinctions and are still living today.

Hagfish and lampreys

Hagfish and lampreys are jawless fish that look like eels and snakes. They have single-tail fins and do not have scales on their body. They are scavengers and can feed on other large fish by attaching themselves to the fish's body. They can absorb nutrients and juices through their skin. Lampreys have a good immune system, which might have protected them from becoming extinct. When captured, hagfish secrete a slimy mucous in large amounts as a defence tactic. Such defence mechanisms have helped these fish species survive till now.

Lamprey

Dunkleosteus

Dunkleosteus were fearsome jawed fish that lived during the ancient times. They were heavily armoured and were probably the largest predators, about 9 m long and weighed about 3 or 4 tonnes. Instead of teeth, *Dunkleosteus* possessed two long and sharp bony plates in their mouth. They could bite with an enormous force using their massive and powerful jaws.

Prehistoric sharks

Prehistoric sharks were the first jawed fish with razor-sharp teeth. They belonged to the group chondrichthians that had skeletons made of an elastic substance called cartilage.

Facts

- *Pterichthyodes* were placoderms and had wing-like appendages instead of fins.
- *Dunkleosteus* had a powerful suction technique that allowed them to pull its prey into their mouth in much less than a second.

What is a fish with a cartilaginous skeleton called?

Osteichthyes

Osteichthyes are fish with bony skeletons. Their skeleton is calcified and is harder and stronger than the cartilaginous skeleton of chondrichthians. Osteichthyes have scales on the surface of their skin, paired fins, paired gill openings with gill covers, a pair of nostrils and a swim bladder. They are classified into lobe-finned and ray-finned fish. About 95 per cent of all the modern fish are Osteichthyes.

Coelacanths

Coelacanths are large lobe-finned, deep-sea fish. They have an oil-filled tube called notochord, which serves as a backbone and a rostral organ in the snout for sensing preys. They have a small brain and paired nostrils linked to the mouth, which could be used for breathing. Coelacanths were related to the first tetrapods, the fish that developed fin-like legs and could move on land.

Fish with bony skeletons are called _____.

Lungfish

Lungfish are one of the primitive fish that still exist today. They have a snake-like body and long and thin pectoral and pelvic fins. They can breathe through gills as well as lungs and feed on small sea animals. Lungfish secrete a slimy liquid from their skin that covers their body and retains moisture. This helps them to stay out of water for many days.

▲ *Cheirolepis*

Cheirolepis

Cheirolepis were prehistoric ray-finned fish. These predators were about 55 cm long and had small scales on their skin. They also had large eyes with a sharp vision and well-developed fins that gave them pace and steadiness. Cheirolepis had several piercing teeth and were avid eaters. They could swallow preys up to two-thirds their size. They used to feed on agnathans, acanthodians, placoderms and sometimes the members of their own species.

Facts

- Coelacanths were believed to have gone extinct about 65 million years ago. However, they were discovered once again in 1938 in South Africa.
- Some lungfish can use their pelvic fins as hind legs to walk.

Anatomy of Fish - I

The structure of fish helps them to live and survive underwater. Almost all fish have a streamlined body, brain, heart and gills. All the parts of the body carry out different functions.

Backbone

Fish are vertebrates and their backbone starts from the skull and reaches the tail. Their ribs are attached to the backbone and shield the internal organs. The bones also support muscles and give fish their shape. The spinal cord is inside the backbone and connects the brain to the nerves, muscles and the various organs. Sensory information is passed from the body to the brain, and instructions are passed from the brain to the rest of the body.

Brain

Fish have a small brain as compared to their body size. The brain has large lobes for smell and sight. It interprets all the sensory information. They also have ears inside their head for hearing sound. Some fish like sharks have larger brains and are highly intelligent. They use their intelligence for hunting preys.

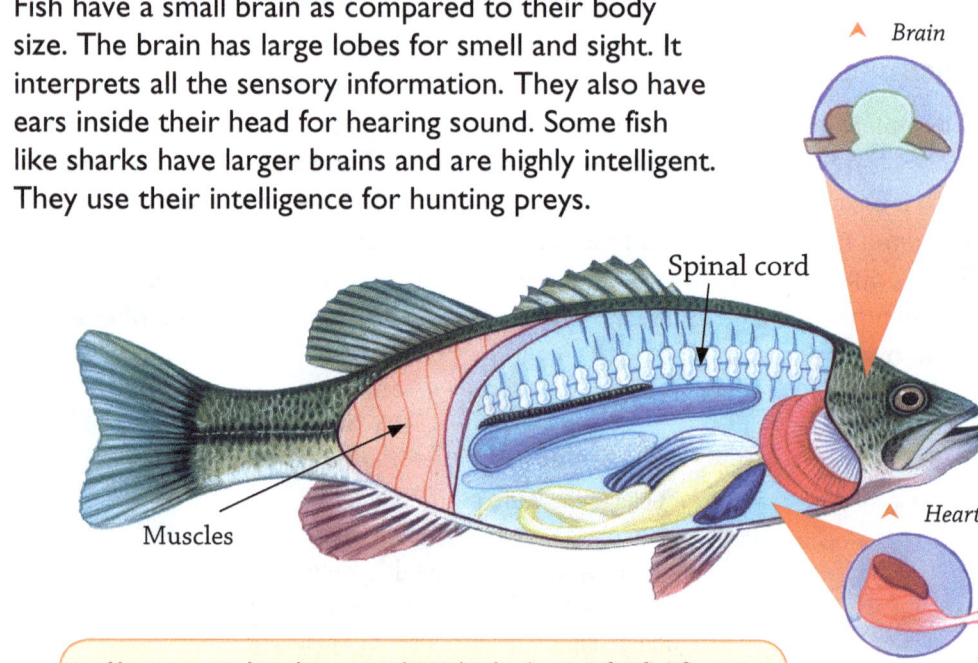

▲ *Brain*

Spinal cord

Muscles

▲ *Heart*

How many chambers are there in the heart of a fish?

Heart

The heart of a fish has two chambers—thin-walled atrium and muscular ventricle. The heart pumps blood into the atrium and passes to the ventricle, which then contracts and forces blood through the network of capillaries in the gills. Blood then reaches each and every cell in the body and comes back to the heart.

Swim bladder

Fish are able to swim underwater without sinking due to the presence of an air bladder or a swim bladder inside them. The swim bladder is filled with air and provides the necessary buoyancy for fish to remain afloat. It lets fish sleep in water without the fear of sinking.

Lateral line

The lateral line lies just below the surface of the skin and is filled with a jelly-like liquid containing many sensory nerve endings. It allows a fish to sense what is happening around it. A fish can sense pressure, change in temperature, vibration, movement and sounds.

Facts

- Trout fish need lots of oxygen and are found in colder waters because of the high level of oxygen present there.
- Many fish have chemoreceptors that give them an extraordinary sense of taste and smell.

Anatomy of Fish - II

Fish are cold-blooded aquatic animals. They have all the necessary adaptations that make them capable of living in shallow waters as well as deep dark waters of the benthic zones (lowest levels of a water body). Almost all fish have scaly skin, fins and tails as well as gills to breathe oxygen.

Fins

Fish have fins to help them steer through water. They are the appendages that help fish in forward movement, swimming, floating, keeping balance, changing directions and reducing the rolling motion during swimming. Pectoral fins, pelvic fins, dorsal fins and the caudal fin are the different types of fins that fish possess.

Colour and scales

Fish are colourful animals. Their colours play a vital role in camouflaging them. Fish also have scales on their body for protection. They have a layer of slime over the scales, which helps them to move fast and keep germs off their skin. The scales on the skin of a putterfish look like spikes when the fish is puffed up.

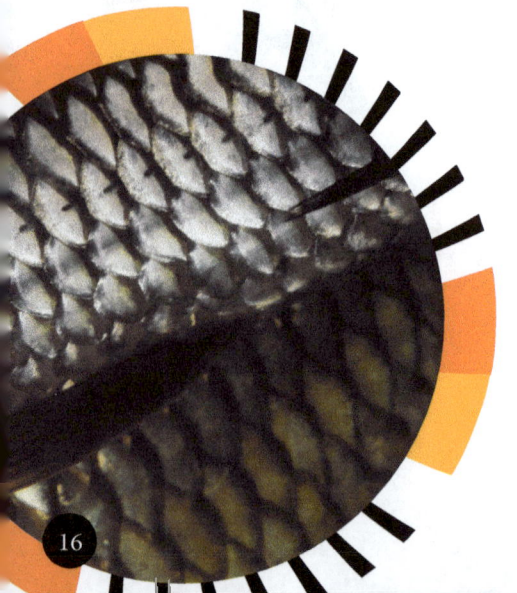

Gills

Fish have gills instead of lungs to aid them in the process of respiration. Gills are present in other aquatic animals as well. The exchange of gases takes place in the gills—they take in dissolved oxygen from water and expel carbon dioxide and other wastes. A fish takes in water from its mouth and pumps it across the gills by moving the gill covers.

Facts

- Fish can only live in gradually varying water temperatures. They will die if the water temperature changes all of a sudden.
- Though it is understood that fish do not sense pain, some experiments have shown that they may exhibit pain responses in specific situations.

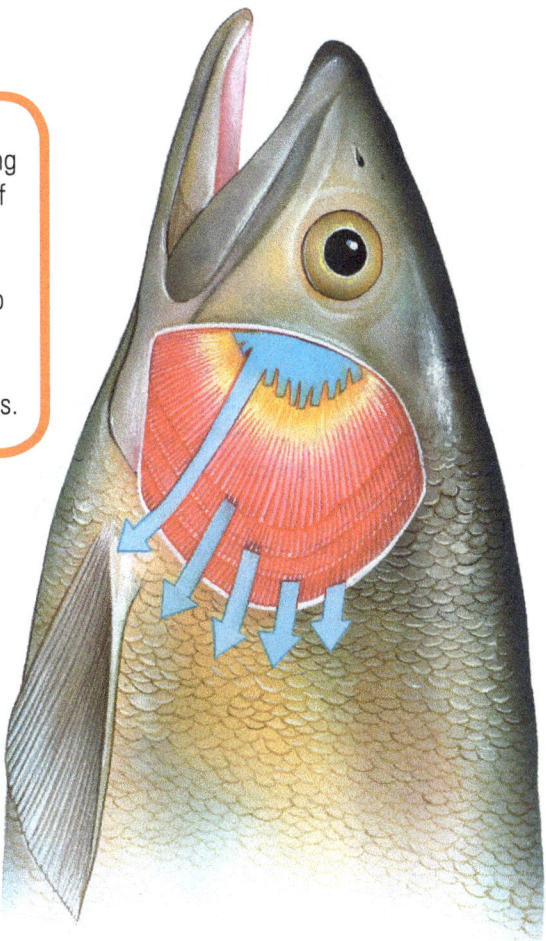

Are fish warm-blooded or cold-blooded animals?

Sharks

Sharks are the most feared creatures on Earth. They have been swimming in the world's oceans even before the age of dinosaurs. Some people call them 'monsters of the deep' because they hunt their prey with an unmatched ferocity. They are intelligent sea animals with a large brain and good memory.

Body

Sharks have a muscular, streamlined body with a cartilaginous skeleton, and their skin is covered with small tooth-like scales called denticles. They have as many as seven pairs of gills to aid them in breathing. They do not have swim bladders but their livers are filled with an oil that provides them with the necessary buoyancy. However, sharks still need to keep swimming to remain afloat.

Babies

Baby sharks are called pups. Though most sharks give birth to live young, some are known to lay eggs. Those sharks that give birth to babies are called viviparous sharks. Hammerhead sharks and whale sharks are viviparous sharks. Mother sharks don't care for their babies, and they can even feed on their own pups. So the pups swim away from their mothers as fast as they can to save their lives.

Teeth

Sharks have rows of long, sharp and serrated teeth pointing inward. At a time, some species can have 3,000 teeth in their mouth. The teeth are constantly being replaced, and a shark may use as many as 30,000 teeth in its lifetime.

A shark's skeleton is made of_____.

Senses

Sharks are also known as 'swimming noses' for their excellent sense of smell. The part of a shark's brain responsible for detecting smell is twice as large as the rest. Sharks can detect odour in water from almost a mile away. They also have lateral lines on both sides of the body that help them sense movement in water. Sharks also have sharp hearing and vision.

Facts

- Sharks can sense electric signals with the help of small sensory jelly-filled pores called ampullae of Lorenzini, located on their snout.
- Those sharks that live deep in the ocean have a better eyesight than the other sharks.

Predatory Sharks

Sharks are known to rule the underwater food chain. Their highly developed senses help them to detect prey from a great distance. Some of the most ferocious sharks are great white sharks, hammerheads, whale sharks and reef sharks.

Hammerhead sharks

Hammerhead sharks have a unique head that is shaped like a hammer. The great hammerheads are the largest of all hammerheads. They also have bigger brains than most sharks. Their eyes and nostrils are at the far end of their head, which helps them scan a larger area of the ocean floor. They usually hunt near the bottom of the sea and use their broad head to pin down the prey, including stingrays, squid, lobsters and shellfish.

Which sharks are the largest of all sharks?

Whale sharks

Whale sharks are the biggest of all sharks. They swim slowly with their mouth wide open, eating small fish and plankton. Their feeding mechanism is called filter feeding. They are docile creatures and are not as aggressive as other sharks.

Facts

- The angelfish is a hammerhead shark's friendly cleaner as it picks up parasites from the shark's skin and the interiors of its mouth. The shark does not eat its cleaner.
- In February 2012, some Pakistani fishermen caught a giant whale shark that was 10.9 m long and weighed about 7,000 kg.

Great white sharks

Great white sharks are one of deadliest predators in the ocean. They have a blue-grey upper body and are named after their white underbelly. They can grow up to 6.4 m in length and can weigh up to 2,268 kg. They can even jump out of water like whales for catching their prey. This is called breaching. They mainly feed on seals, dolphins, sea lions and penguins. Sometimes they can also eat other sharks.

Reef sharks

The sharks that live near coral reefs are called reef sharks. Whitetip, blacktip and Caribbean reef sharks are a few of the species of reef sharks. Whitetip and blacktip reef sharks are called so because the tip of their fins and tails are white and black, respectively.

Rays and Skates

Rays and skates do not look like fish at all but belong to the group of cartilaginous fish along with sharks. They have a flat body, five pairs of gills, a long trailing tail and wing-like pectoral fins. They usually spend their life on the ocean floor, feeding on mollusks, crustaceans, worms and sometimes small fish. Like sharks, they can also sense electric signals.

Stingrays

Stingrays are known for their sharp stings, which they use to ward off the enemy when they feel threatened. They have a long, slim, whip-like tail armed with saw-like, venomous spines. Both the venom and the spine can be dangerous. Stingrays commonly live in the shallow coastal waters of temperate seas.

Name the smallest skate in the world.

Facts

- Skates lay fertilized eggs in their egg case, which are also known as a 'mermaid's purse'.
- Electric rays have cells called electrocytes in their body, which generate electric currents when stimulated.

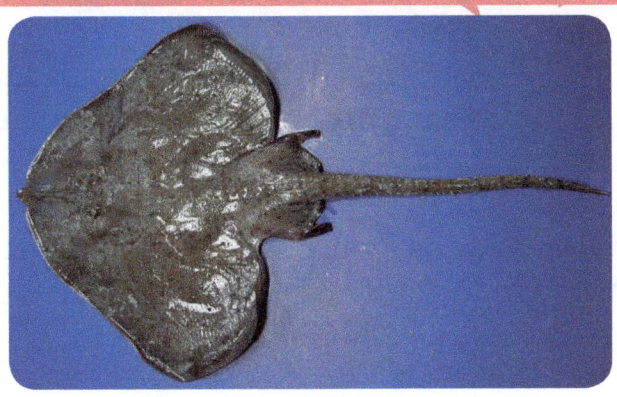

Skates

The mouth and gills of skates are located on their underbelly, whereas their eyes are located on the top of their head. Most skates have a scaly skin and spiracles on the top of their head for taking in water, which is then passed through the gills. The clearnose skate is the smallest skate and weighs about 1-2 kg.

Manta rays

Manta rays are the largest rays and weigh about 1,200 to 1,400 kg. They are related to devil rays because of the horn-like fins on the top of their head. They like to swim near the surface unlike most rays and can even jump out of water. Manta rays are solitary animals.

Venomous Fish

There are many venomous fish in the oceans that are not as big as the master predator sharks but are equally deadly. They use their venom for hunting and some use it as an offensive weapon just the way snakes do. Unlike snakes that have fangs, venomous fish bear sharp spikes. Some of them are bottom-dwellers, whereas some live in the tropical shores.

Lionfish

Lionfish are one of the most spectacular-looking fish in the world. They have vivid stripes on the body and posses extremely flamboyant pectoral fins. Their magnificent dorsal fins have spines all over, which are used for injecting venom into the enemy. The sting of a lionfish can be extremely painful to humans but is rarely fatal. Lionfish are also very swift and highly camouflaged, which helps them to look for their preys.

Stonefish

Stonefish are one of the most venomous fish in the world. These fish have a row of 13 needle-like dorsal spines on their back that are used to inject venom when the fish feel threatened. They usually live on the seabed among stones or in rock crevices and are perfectly camouflaged. When a shoal of small fish swim by, a stonefish opens its mouth and gobbles them down within a fraction of a second.

Stargazer

Stargazers bury themselves in the seabed and blend completely with the surroundings. Their head is the only part that remains above the ground as these ambush predators lie camouflaged. Stargazers have two large venom-inducing spines above their pectoral fins. They are even capable of producing great electric shocks from a special organ located behind the eyes.

Facts
- The venom of a dead fish remains effective for up to 24 hours after the fish has died.
- Stargazers use the appendage on their lower lip that looks like a worm to attract their prey.

Which fish are capable of producing electric shocks?

Unusual Fish

There are certain incredible sea creatures that don't look like fish at all but are actually fish. Seahorses, sea dragons and pipefish are some of the most unusual fish. All these fish are a visual delight. They live in seaweeds, kelps and beds of seagrass in tropical and temperate waters around the world.

Seahorses

Seahorses are named for their extraordinary equine shape. Like monkeys, seahorses have a prehensile tail that can wrap around and take hold of objects. Unlike other fish, they swim in an upright position. According to scientists, there are more than 45 species of seahorses, some of which are only 2.5 cm long. Male seahorses are larger than the females. Along with sea dragons, they are one of the near-threatened species.

Facts

- Unlike most other fish, seahorses mate for life.
- Seahorses do not have teeth and a stomach. They must eat constantly because food passes through their digestive system very quickly.

Sea dragons

Sea dragons are one of the most beautiful and ornately camouflaged fish in the world. Leafy sea dragons, ruby sea dragons and weedy sea dragons are the three types of sea dragons. They eat small sea lice, plankton and mysids. Leafy sea dragons are brown to yellow in colour and have magnificent leaf-like appendages all over the body. Weedy sea dragons have less striking appendages and are generally reddish in colour with yellow polka dots and ruby sea dragons are dark red with stumpy lobes.

Pipefish

How many species of seahorses are there?

Pipefish are long and slender and have an elongated, tube-like snout with a small toothless mouth. They come in a wide range of colours and patterns, and some of the species can change colours according to thier surroundings. Almost all male pipefish have a special pouch like marsupials to carry their eggs, which are deposited by females.

Aquarium Fish

Some fish are so beautiful that people love to keep them as pets. They don't need grooming or our company all the time. Some popular pet fish are extremely robust and make great pets. Goldfish, tetra fish, barbs, betta fish and guppies are some of the popular aquarium fish around the world.

Tetra fish

Tetra fish are small freshwater fish. They are loving and peaceful. Tetras live in schools to guard each other and to find food. They might feel sad and anxious if kept alone in an aquarium. Therefore, it is best to keep a small school of tetras.

Goldfish

Goldfish belong to the largest family of fish in the world, which has more than 2,400 species. The reason for their popularity as pets is their gregarious nature. They are playful and have strong learning and social skills. Goldfish can even distinguish between colours, sounds and shapes. They can also recognize their owners.

Betta fish

Betta fish, also known as the Siamese fighting fish, are one of the most attractive and colourful fish. They feed on small worms, insects, insect larvae, shrimps and carrion. They have gills to breathe in water and a special organ called labyrinth behind their head to breathe out of water. Male bettas have more glitzy fins than female bettas. They fight to defend their territory.

Facts

- Goldfish first appeared as pets in China.
- Male bettas are known to flare their gills, twist their bodies and spread their fins to attract a female.

Among goldfish and barbs, which fish have rows of teeth like shark?

Barbs

Barbs are freshwater tropical fish. They feed on other smaller fish, bloodworms, insects and some aquatic plants. Also, they have rows of teeth, just like sharks. They are very dominant and ferocious in nature. Some barbs are fin nippers. They enjoy nipping fins of fish that have long and trail-like fins. To keep their aggressive behaviour, barbs should be housed with other barbs.

Coral Reef Fish

Coral reef fish live in close proximity of coral reefs. Coral reefs support a large array of sea animals and are one of the important ecosystems of the planet. Some of the most common reef fish are clown fish, angelfish, tang fish and the Moorish idol.

Tang fish

Tang fish are relatives of surgeon fish and are brightly coloured. They mainly graze on algae, grass and other plants with the help of their protruding short snout. They have spines on their tail. Tangs also have large dorsal and caudal fins extending from the most part of their body. A blue tang can change its colour from light blue to dark purple.

Angelfish

Angelfish are one of the most beautiful of all reef creatures. They come in vivid colours and have large scales. Angelfish also have a protruding spine on the lower edge of the gill covers. Their brilliantly patterned body helps them to hide amid the colourful coral reefs. These fish are shy, peaceful and territorial. They eat sponges, algae and small crustaceans.

Moorish idols

Moorish idols have striking, long-flowing dorsal fins and a black tail. As babies, they occasionally form schools but prefer to live alone or in pairs when they grow up. Like butterfly fish. They are diurnal fish and spend the night in the reefs. Sponges are their favourite food.

Clown fish

Clown fish are small, bright-coloured fish. They are also called anemone fish because they live among sea anemones. Clown fish share a symbiotic relationship with the anemones. They help each other survive in the ocean. Clown fish clean the anemone by eating algae and the leftover of other fish and defend their territory, while sea anemones provide clown fish food and a safe home.

Coral reefs are living creatures. True or false?

Facts

- Clown fish have a greasy mucous covering on their body that protects them from the stings of sea anemones.
- Moorish idols are the only living members of their family.

Camouflage Fish

Camouflage is a hiding technique used by some creatures so that they blend in with the surroundings and become unnoticeable. It can be achieved by altering the shape, colour or behaviour. Many living organisms adopt such camouflage behaviours to ward off predators and to catch preys.

Anglerfish

Anglerfish come in various shades of brown, grey and black. They dwell at the bottom of the sea and possess bioluminescence. The female anglerfish lies motionless on the ground and uses its extremely long and luminescent dorsal spine as a fishing pole to attract its prey. When the prey comes close enough, it pierces the prey with its pointed, fang-like teeth and devours it.

Facts

- Toadfish can live out of water for long periods.
- The male anglerfish is quite smaller than the female.

Toadfish

Toadfish are benthic zone predators. They have a slimy, scaleless body; a flat head; a round nose; a big mouth; a plump belly; and fan-like pectoral fins. Their physical appearance, dull colour and colour-changing abilities camouflage them completely. Toadfish lie on the sea floor as they wait for their prey. They are poisonous and croak and grunt to attract their prey.

Crocodile fish

Crocodile fish blend remarkably into the surrounding environment and lie on the ocean floor in wait for their prey. They have a crocodile-like snout and fluorescent green crisscross markings on their body. They even have some frilly iris lappets on the eyes, which improve their camouflage. Baby crocodile fish are entirely black but acquire colours as they grow old.

> Name the fish that uses its dorsal fin as bait.

Trumpet fish

Trumpet fish are masters of camouflage. They hang upside down and remain motionless to appear like corals or weeds. They can also change colours and swim upright with their long snout downward, which helps them to merge in with the surrounding pipe sponges, sea fans and sea whips. As the prey passes by, a trumpet fish sucks it with great power.

Balloon Fish

There are some fish in the wild that can blow themselves up with air or water like balloons. They do so in order to protect themselves and to ward off predators. If not threatened, they look like ordinary fish. Porcupine fish, pufferfish and boxfish are some of the balloon fish. All these fish are poisonous and slow swimmers.

Pufferfish

Pufferfish are small fish with smooth skin and the ability to blow up their body with water or air. Some pufferfish are pale coloured, while some are brightly coloured. They can change colours to blend into the surroundings. They have a long, narrow body with a round head. Pufferfish belong to the family of fish that have four teeth. Their teeth are fused together and are used to crush the prey. They are supposed to be one of the most poisonous animals in the world.

Porcupine fish

The porcupine fish looks like an ordinary fish with spines until it is threatened. When the fish is afraid, it swallows water, which makes it round like a ball. As the body inflates, its spines stand out. The needle-like spines can be as long as 5 cm. Porcupine fish have large eyes and plate-like teeth in the upper and lower jaws for crushing food like mollusks, shellfish and prawns.

Boxfish

Boxfish have a squarish body enclosed in a shell of bony plates. These slow-moving fish are easily stressed. When under stress, they release a toxin that can kill the nearby sea animals. This group of fish includes cowfish and trunkfish.

Facts

- Pufferfish is called fugu in Japan, where it is an expensive food item. The fish is prepared by only trained and licensed chefs.
- Pufferfish are able to blow themselves up to several times their normal size.

The _____ eat pufferfish as a delicious meal.

Small Sea Predators

Oceans and seas are full of fearsome marine predators. Sharks and whales are two of the most frightening hunters in the world. But they are not the only predators in the sea. The marine world is full of small carnivorous fish that feed on other fish and can be fatal to humans. Piranhas are called small monsters of the sea.

Barracudas

Barracudas are lean, predatory fish. They have a long snout and pointed mouth with knife-like teeth. They are silver with black blotches, criss-cross lines and yellow tail and fins. Some barracudas grow to be about 1.8 m and weigh about 23 kg. They are more aggressive than most sharks and attack the prey with great speed. They are swift swimmers and can swim at the speed of 40 km per hour. They attack almost all types of fish that cross their way.

Facts

- A large group of barracudas is called a battery.
- Needlefish are easily excited when they sight artificial lights.

The _____ is the most aggressive piranha

Piranhas

Piranhas are fierce hunters that are always on the hunt. They hunt caimans and other sea animals in large schools of up to 100 fish. They have a large round head, small but powerful jaws lined with numerous pointed teeth that fit together like a zipper and large eyes that provide them with sharp vision. The red-bellied piranha is the most ferocious of all piranhas.

Needlefish

Needlefish are small but fierce hunters. They eat other fish and are extremely fearful. They have a long, slender body with an elongated snout and a beak-like mouth filled with razor-sharp teeth. Needlefish are usually seen swimming near the surface. They can jump out of the water with great speed and attack people on board a ship. Their sharp beak is capable of inserting deep into the flesh and often breaking off in the process, killing the victim almost instantly.

Fast Swimming Fish

Oceans and seas are home to some of the fastest swimming fish, which include tuna, swordfish and sailfish. They are hunters and are known to chase their prey at high speeds. These fast swimmers have a pointed head, torpedo-shaped body and large crescent-shaped tail, which impel them powerfully through the water.

Sailfish

Sailfish are one of the fastest swimmers in the ocean. They have sail-like dorsal fins stretching across their back and an elongated bill. Sailfish can sprint up to 110 km per hour. They are bluish grey in colour with stripes and can even change colours. Sailfish keep their sail folded when swimming but raise it if they are chasing preys to make themselves appear much larger. While swimming in groups, they use their sail to herd a school of fish.

Facts

- Swordfish can lay millions of eggs at a time, which are fertilized outside their body.
- Bluefin tunas are known to make extraordinarily long migrations. Some bluefins travel from North American waters to European waters several times a year.

_____ are warm-blooded tunas.

Swordfish

Swordfish are named for their long, flat and pointed sword-like bill, which can reach about a third of their body length. Swordfish can travel at a speed of 97 km per hour to chase preys. They can move rapidly in water zones where the temperatures vary greatly. They have the ability to heat up their eyes and brain with the help of special tissues near their eyes. They use their sharp bill as a weapon to slash larger preys.

Tunas

Tunas are fast swimmers and are capable of swimming at speeds up to 69 km per hour. They are voracious eaters and can eat up to 10 times their body weight. Almost all fish have white flesh, but tunas' flesh varies from pink to red. Atlantic bluefin tunas are warm-blooded and live in cold as well as tropical waters. They can even retract their dorsal and pectoral fins into slots to maintain speed and endurance.

Schooling Fish

Some fish are very social and like to swim together in large groups called schools or shoals. Staying together keeps them safe from predators, which might find it hard to catch a single fish. The schooling fish are usually silver in colour because of the reflective scales on their body that act like mirrors. Their shiny surface also works as a camouflage.

Herrings

Herrings are beautiful, silver-coloured fish. They have a small head, a sleek and slender body and a dorsal fin. Herrings don't have a lateral line. They swim near the surface and feed on plankton, fish larvae and small crustaceans. They keep their mouth open while swimming in order to filter plankton through their gills.

What is the other name of glassfish?

Snappers

Snappers live among the tropical and subtropical waters of all oceans and seas. They can grow up to a length of 90 cm and come in a wide range of colours, including yellow with blue or black stripes, red, greyish silver, etc. They have a large mouth filled with sharp canine teeth for eating crustaceans. Bluestripe snappers live in close association with yellowfin goatfish that resemble the snappers. This relationship protects the snappers from attacks as predators would target goatfish, which are a tastier meal than the snappers.

Glassfish

Glassfish are small fish that have a strikingly transparent body. Their bone structure and internal organs are visible through their clear body. Glassfish are found in fresh water and in seas, along the coasts and the river mouth. The schools of glassfish stay together during the day and disperse during at night to feed. Glassfish are also called glass perch.

Facts

- Flying fish are school fish that can leap out of water at a speed of 56 km per hour. They can fly above the surface for about half a minute.
- Mangrove snappers, one of the smallest snappers, do not grow beyond 45 cm in length.

Strange Looking Fish

Some fish are known for their bizarre appearance. They do not look like fish at all but share all the characteristics of fish. Frogfish, blob sculpins and eels are some of the very strange-looking fish.

Frogfish

Frogfish are a type of anglerfish. They are brightly coloured and covered with loose flesh that looks like floating algae. Like anglerfish, they lie motionless on the sea floor and use their long dorsal fin as bait to catch preys. Frogfish are also poor swimmers and use their fins to walk and climb rocks.

Frogfish are a type of _____.

Blob sculpins

Blob sculpins or blobfish are deep-sea fish. They do not have muscles and bones. Their body is made up of a gel-like liquid that helps them float above the sea floor. Blobfish hardly swim and wait for their preys to pass by. They feed on sea urchins, sea crabs and mollusks.

Eels

Eels live in marine water and fresh water around the world. They are snake-shaped fish with a smooth, slimy and scaleless skin. Eels have a body designed to slither through small cracks in the ocean floor, rocks and crevices and among corals. They are of different colours ranging from black, brown to red, yellow, green or blue. Baby eels are transparent.

Facts

- Eels can swim forward as well as backward.
- Electric eels can generate an electric charge of 600 volts to keep predators at bay.

Glossary

Abundance: a very large quantity of something

Ancient: very old or primitive

Appendage: limb

Bioluminescence: the ability in certain deep-sea creatures to produce light

Bizarre: very strange or odd

Buoyancy: the ability to float

Calcified: hardened with the deposition of calcium carbonate

Caudal fin: also called tail fin, it acts as a motor as it propels the fish forward and creates speed

Crustacean: an aquatic organism with many legs and a hard shell for protection

Diurnal: during the day

Dorsal fin: an unpaired fin on the back of a fish or whale

Ecosystem: natural environment of organisms that interact with each other

Extinct: something that is dead and no longer exists

Flamboyant: brightly coloured

Gregarious: fond of living in groups

Immune System: a system inside the body of an organism that helps it fight off germs and infections

Incredible: hard to believe or unbelievable

Luminescent: a substance emitting light

Magnificent: very beautiful or impressive

Marsupial: an animal that carries its baby in a pouch attached to its skin

Pectoral fin: each of a pair of fins located on either side just behind a fish's head; help in maintaining balance during locomotion

Pelvic fin: each of a pair of fins on the underside of a fish's body; help in controlling direction

Placoderm: an armoured prehistoric fish

Plankton: a very small organism that drifts in waterbodies

Predator: an animal that feeds on other animals

Prey: an animal that is eaten by predators

Scavenger: an organism that feeds on the dead remains of other organisms

Sea Anemone: a plant-like, poisonous, carnivorous sea animal with tentacles

Symbiotic Relationship: a relationship between two organisms of different species that benefits both of them in some way

Tetrapod: an animal with four limbs

Threatened Species: those species of animals that are on the verge of becoming endangered

Answers

Page No. 8	True
Page No. 11	Chondrichthians
Page No. 12	Osteichthyes
Page No. 14	Two
Page No. 17	Cold-blooded
Page No. 19	Cartilage
Page No. 20	Whale shark
Page No. 22	Clearnose skate
Page No. 25	Stargazers
Page No. 27	More than 45
Page No. 29	Barbs
Page No. 31	True
Page No. 33	Anglerfish
Page No. 35	Japanese
Page No. 36	Red-bellied piranha
Page No. 38	Atlantic bluefin tunas
Page No. 40	Glass perch
Page No. 42	Anglerfish

AMPHIBIANS

Introduction

Amphibians are a unique category of animals that have adapted to live both on land and in water. 'Amphibios', translated from the Greek, means 'living a double life'. Most amphibians start life in water and later move to land as adults. They go through a series of transformations to enable themselves to live in two diverse habitats. This process is known as metamorphosis.

Amphibians evolved around 365 million years ago and were the first vertebrates to have inhabited the Earth. Lobe-finned fish are their predecessors, while reptiles are their successors. These slippery, slimy creatures can be found in diverse climates and environments. The tiny amphibians are usually found in wet and watery environments and do not inhabit marine habitats at all. The amphibian family has intrigued scientists with their unusual features, adaptations and abilities.

Features

Amphibians are vertebrates that can live both on land and in water. A typical amphibian starts out as a larva in water. During this stage, it breathes through its gills. As it matures into an adult, it begins to breathe through its lungs. However, some amphibian species do not pass through the tadpole stage and some others retain their gills throughout their lives.

Eyesight

Amphibians' eyes are capable of functioning both on land and in water. They are equipped with upper and lower eyelids to avoid the surface of their eyes from drying. Some terrestrial frogs also have lacrimal glands. Frogs only perceive moving objects with their eyes while everything else blends with the background. Most caecilians are blind.

Amphibians are warm-blooded animals. True/false?

Cold-blooded animals

Amphibians are cold-blooded animals, which means that their body temperature depends on the outside temperature. These animals derive heat from their surroundings. It is for this reason that amphibians are very active in warm climates and environments but are lethargic when they are exposed to low temperatures.

Hearing

Amphibians have a great hearing capacity. They do not have external ears. However, they have thin disks of membranes located on their body that serve as eardrums. Sound waves in the environment cause vibrations that are transmitted to the brain.

Locomotion

Most amphibians are tetrapods. The limbs of amphibians can function well both on land and in water. Their front legs are different from most other tetrapods. Their legs are suited for walking on land, swimming in water, climbing trees, constructing nests, etc.

Facts

- Some burrowing amphibians have 'seismic' hearing capabilities. They perceive their environment by sensing vibrations through their lower jaw.
- A frog shuts its eyes while leaping to avoid any possible traumas.

Evolution

Amphibians were the first vertebrates that left water to live on land around 360 million years ago. Over the next 125 million years, amphibians faced little competition from other vertebrates and evolved into as many as 3 major groups. The fossilised remains of the earliest-known amphibians indicate that they evolved from lobe-finned fish. These fish developed an early form of lungs and a moveable pair of fins.

Devonian period

The earliest type of amphibian is believed to be the ichthyostega, which lived during the late Devonian Period. It had lungs and legs that helped it walk. This allowed it to live on land for extended periods and search for food. Since these amphibians were tetrapods, they could search for other water bodies if the ones they lived in dried up.

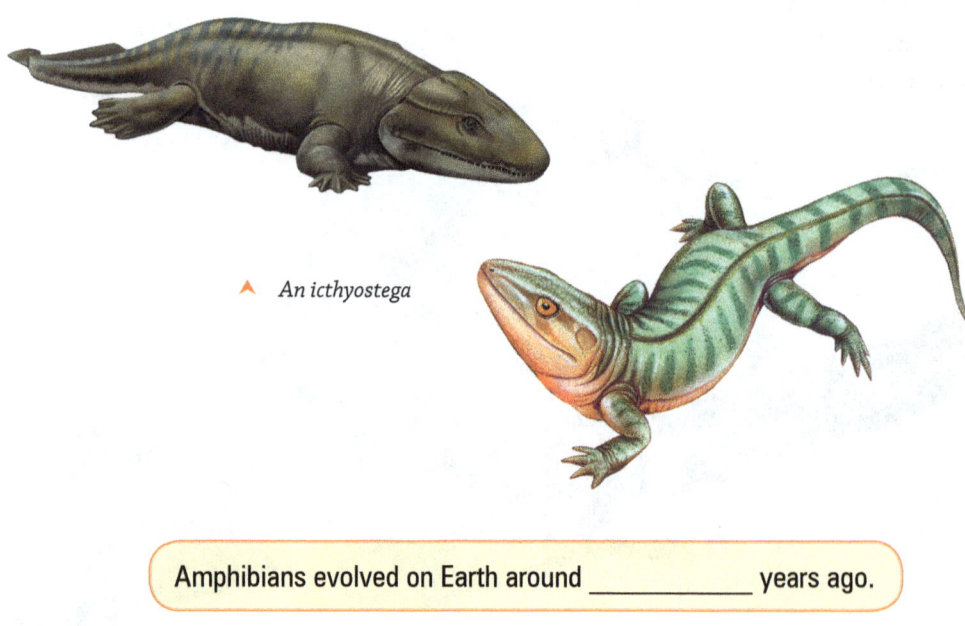

▲ *An icthyostega*

Amphibians evolved on Earth around _____ years ago.

Carboniferous period

During this time amphibians adapted to life on land. They evolved short hands and feet with five toes. Their nostrils and eardrums developed more. Their backbones also grew stronger, which enabled their bodies to grow. Rhachitomes were the dominant amphibians of this period. They were a highly diversified group, differing in size, lifestyle and features.

Archegosaurus decheni, a primitive crocodile-like amphibian.

Facts

- It is believed that the earliest amphibians lived most of their lives in water.
- The oldest amphibian fossil remains appear like a fish with muscular fins.

Permian period

Before this period, amphibians were the dominant group of animals. They had large bodies and mostly fed on insects. Vast expanses of land were underwater and provided a suitable habitat for them. However, by the end of this period, land became drier and some species of amphibians that adapted well to this environment evolved into early reptiles.

Classification

Amphibians can be classified into three main groups, each with their distinct characteristics. These three groups are: newts and salamanders, frogs and toads, and caecilians.

Newts and salamanders

Newts and salamanders form a group of amphibians that consists of 760 species. These amphibians have a slender body, a long tail and usually two pairs of limbs. Unlike frogs and toads, newts and salamanders do not croak or produce loud sounds. Among all amphibians, this group most resembles the earliest fossils of amphibians.

Caecilians

This group of amphibians consists of large worms that lack limbs. There are more than 200 species of amphibians that belong to this group. Caecilians live in tropical forests and freshwater sediments. They are aquatic in nature and are found in Africa, South Asia and America.

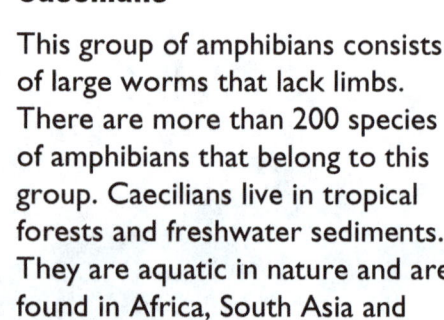

Toads and frogs

Toads and frogs are tailless amphibians. They form the biggest group of amphibians with 7,300 species. They are different from the other amphibians, since they reproduce through external fertilization. Though toads and frogs are part of the same group, they have different characteristics.

Facts

- A glass frog lays its eggs hanging from a branch over a pond. The tadpoles fall directly into the water after hatching.
- Caecilians are the least-known type of amphibians, since they stay hidden underground for most of the time.

Which amphibians are tailless?

Skin

Amphibians have a thin skin resembling a semi-transparent fabric. Their skin is smooth, unlike that of reptiles, which have dry, scaly skin. Amphibians can even absorb water through their skin. They stay near water or wet environments because they have to keep their skin moist. Adult amphibians breathe through their skin.

Sensitive organ

Amphibians' skin also functions as a sensitive organ for perceiving outside information. Some amphibians, such as the African clawed frogs, have sensitive receptors on their skin. They have small organs that look like tiny hollows with microscopic hair. These hair alert the frog to the slightest displacement in the water, such as the movement of a tiny water insect.

Where are wood frogs found?

Moulting

Almost all amphibians undergo seasonal moults, replacing their entire skin. The marsh frog sheds its entire skin starting from its eyes. Moulting can occur at intervals of less than a week, but the exact time varies among species. The skin that is shed is often swallowed by the animal as the moulting progresses.

Frogs with different skin

Wood frogs are among the few frogs that can be found in Alaska and above the Arctic Circle. As the temperature drops below freezing each winter, wood frogs go into deep hibernation. Their heartbeat stops, and small ice crystals start forming on their skin. They can survive in a frozen state due to the high glycogen level in their cells. Glass frogs are some of the most fascinating creatures in the world. They have transparent skin and no pigmentation. Their see-through skin enables a clear view of their heart, organs, blood vessels and bones.

Facts

- Amphibians can drink water through their skin.
- The skin of many frogs and salamanders is sensitive to ultraviolet light.

Respiration

Amphibians have a complex respiratory system that functions both on land and in water. They can get oxygen from water as well as air. They have a universal respiratory system that allows them to breathe in the environment they inhabit.

Respiration on land

Adult amphibians breathe on land through their lungs and mouth's mucous membrane. The lungs of amphibians are simple sac-like structures. They do not have a ribcage or muscles to support breathing. They breathe air in and out of the lungs using their mouths as pumps. The bottom of their mouth cavity moves down, and the air is pulled in through the open nostrils. The air is then forced into the lungs through the larynx.

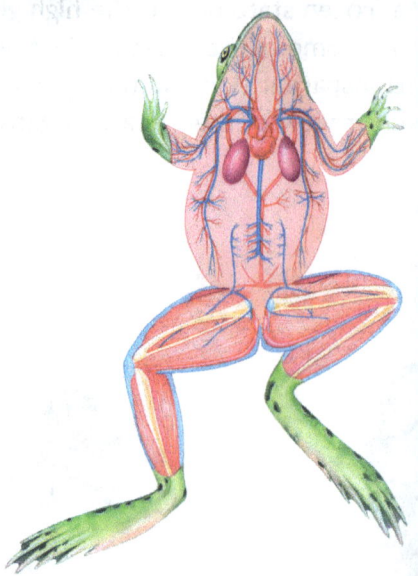

▲ The circulatory system of a frog

> The larvae of amphibians breathe through_____.

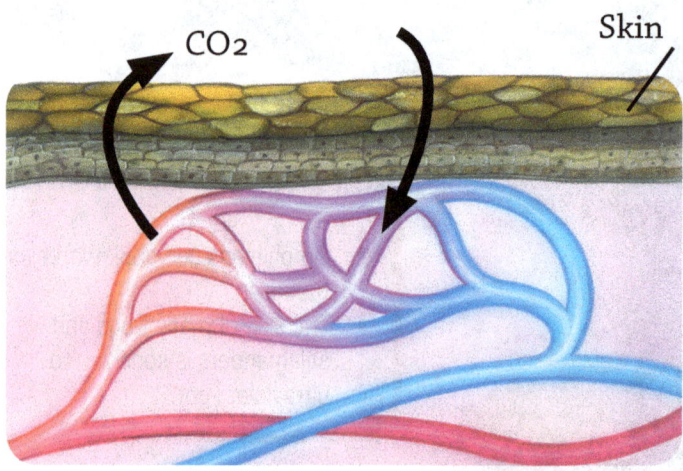

Respiration in water

While amphibians stay in water, they breathe through their skin. Amphibians' larvae and adult-tailed amphibians living in water have gills. Gills are visible externally as tufts on the side of their heads. There are a number of blood vessels near the surface of the skin. When an amphibian is underwater, the skin transmits oxygen straightaway into the bloodstream. Even when the lungs are used, amphibians can take in 50 per cent of the required oxygen if their skin is moist. There are special glands that help keep the skin moist.

Facts

- There are some lungless salamanders that live on land. They neither have gills nor lungs. They take in oxygen and let out carbon dioxide only through their moist skin and the mucous membrane of the mouth.
- The Lake Titicaca frog has wrinkly skin that increases its surface area to enhance the exchange of gases in water with less oxygen.

Food Habits

Amphibians are mostly carnivorous. Aquatic amphibians consume fish, small reptiles and crustaceans, whereas land-bound amphibians consume worms and insects. Each species of amphibians has unique feeding habits. They also have some interesting hunting habits.

Mouth

Most amphibian larvae have tiny teeth. As they grow, most adults retain their teeth. The teeth are used to hold the food in place and not to cut or chew it. All the teeth of an amphibian are the same size and shape. Frogs and toads usually have sticky tongues that they use to catch passing flies. Their tongues is attached to the chin and is covered with mucous to catch prey.

Facts

- An Italian cave salamander can flip out its tongue in 0.01 seconds to catch prey.
- Fire-bellied toads have a fat tongue resembling a disk.

Diet

Small frogs eat whatever is small enough to be eaten. Larger frogs eat small mammals, birds, fish and reptiles. Salamanders mostly feed on insects, worms and slugs. Their food habits may also change when they grow. Caecilians eat things like insect larvae, termites and Earthworms that are found in swampy places, where they live.

Hunting

Salamanders, frogs and toads hunt for insects on the ground. Tropical tree frogs and salamanders catch their prey on branches of trees and shrubs. Many amphibians eat when there is an abundance of insects and live off the accumulated fat in their bodies during hibernation. The hunting activities of amphibians also depend on the outside temperature. When it is cold, they gather in large groups and warm themselves in the sun. When it gets warmer, they go out foraging for food. Common frogs and toads prefer to hunt in the evening and at night.

What do salamanders feed on?

Survival Skills

Amphibians are at risk of being attacked by a wide variety of animals. Predators such as turtles, squirrels and snakes prey on salamanders and frogs. Their eggs and larvae are also eaten by fish, turtles, birds and other frogs. Different amphibians use different survival skills to protect themselves against these predators.

Poison glands

Some amphibians have poison glands on their skin, which deter their predators from eating them. The skin secretes and covers the body with poison. Some amphibians use colours to protect themselves. Most salamanders have glands that secrete a poisonous or foul-tasting fluid on the back of their necks or tails.

▲ *The poison dart frog*

▼ *A camouflaged leopard frog*

Fooling methods

The false-eyed frog has two false eyespots on its back to scare off predators. Some frogs, like the tomato frog, puff themselves up with air to appear too big to be swallowed. Leopard frogs pretend to be dead by keeping very still and holding their breath to avoid being eaten. When a salamander is in danger, it detaches its tail. The detached tail keeps wriggling to distract the predator while it escapes.

Camouflage

Amphibians often use their colour to camouflage into the environment and hide from their predators. Some amphibians can change their colour slowly. Common frogs can change their colour from brownish-red to almost black.

Other defences

The ribbed newt has pointed, needle-like ribs. If attacked, it squeezes its muscles and the pointed ribs pierce through its skin to stab the predator. Some frogs, like the bullfrog, croak loudly to startle predators. Some amphibians urinate to make themselves taste bad to predators and to hide their smell.

Facts

- A peeper tadpole cleans the water in which it lives by feeding on blue-green algae, which is toxic to other fish.
- Some frogs change their colour between the night and day due to the effects of light and moisture on their skin.

Which frog pretends to be dead to escape predators?

Frogs: Characteristics

Frogs and toads form the largest of the three groups of amphibians. They have short bodies, bulging eyes and do not have tails. They are found everywhere except Antarctica. Their skin is soft, smooth and moist, and they normally prefer moist environments.

Locomotion

Frogs are tetrapods with strong and long webbed feet adapted toW jumping and hopping. Toads have short front legs and move on land by leaping across short distances or walking. Frogs have long hind legs with strong muscles that help them jump very high. Their front feet have soft pads, which let them land smoothly. Frogs move in water by pushing their powerful hind legs while the front legs are pressed against the body.

Facts

- Marsupial frogs are those frogs that have a brood pouch.
- The secretions of the Sonoran Desert toad can cause hallucinations among humans.

Singing

Frogs are known for their singing. Not only do they sing with their mouth and nostrils tightly closed but they can even sing underwater. Male frogs sing with special 'vocal pouches' that inflate and deflate. They sing to attract female frogs during the breeding season.

Biggest and smallest

The Goliath frog, found in Cameroon and Equatorial Guinea, is the largest frog on Earth. It can grow up to 33 cm and weigh up to 3 kg. The gold frog of Brazil and the golden litter frog of Cuba are the smallest frogs. They grow up to 1 cm in length and are often smaller than a fingernail.

Name the biggest frog.

Metamorphosis

Most amphibians begin their life in water. They grow underwater and move to land when they are old enough. Amphibians return to the site where they were born to breed and lay eggs. The eggs hatch into larvae, which mature into adults. The larvae go through a process known as metamorphosis during which they completely change.

Eggs and tadpoles

Female frogs lay their eggs in a cluster. Not all the eggs hatch. Some eggs either break up or are consumed by aquatic animals. The eggs hatch after 7–9 days. When the eggs hatch, the tadpoles or larvae come out. Tadpoles don't have tails, legs or a mouth, and they don't look like frogs at all. Tadpoles feed on the egg yolk that is still attached to their body. Young tadpoles have soft, feathery gills outside their body to breathe in water. Gradually, they learn how to swim and feed on algae. After eight weeks, tadpoles grow their hind legs and their gills are covered by skin.

Adult frogs

After 16 weeks, a tadpole looks like a baby frog with a long tail. This froglet eventually completely loses its tail and grows lungs and front legs. It also grows a long tongue to feed on insects. Then, it is an adult frog, which is capable of living outside water.

How many days do frog eggs take to hatch?

Facts

- A female bullfrog lays up to 20,000 eggs at once.
- A batrachologist is a person who studies amphibians.

▲ The female frog lays eggs

▲ An adult frog

◄ Tadpoles develop into froglets

▲ Larvae come out of the eggs

Frogs Habitats

Frogs come in a wide variety of shapes, sizes and colours. There are nearly 3,500 species of frogs living in forests, marshes and even deserts. Frogs eat, move and breed according to their environment.

Tree frogs

Frogs living in trees usually have sticky pads on the tips of their fingers and toes, which help them to stick to plants and trees. Some tree-dwelling frogs, such as the Asian flying frog, have webbing on their front and hind limbs, which allow them to glide between trees in rainforests. They stretch out their webbed feet, which act as an air brake when they hop from one branch to the other.

Facts

- The rocket frog from Africa can jump up to 4.2 high.
- The bullfrog is an aquatic frog that stays completely in water.

Aquatic frogs

The gastric-brooding frog, found in Australia, was an aquatic frog with eyes on the top of its head, which enabled it to float inside the water with its eyes above the water. It used to swallow its eggs and release them from the mouth after they grew past the tadpole stage. The frog could block its gastric juices to allow the rearing of its young ones. It is believed that this frog species is now extinct.

How many types of frog species are there in the world?

Desert frogs

A desert-dwelling frog known as the Catholic frog, found in Australia, fights the drought by burying itself in the sand and emerging only during the rains. Another frog found in the Australian desert, known as the flat-headed frog, also lives in burrows and is known for its ability to store lots of water in its body by assuming a ball-like shape.

Poisonous Frogs and Toads

Many frogs have poison glands in their skin that shoot out poison at predators. Toads often have a puffy-looking pocket at the back of their eyes called the parotid gland that secretes poison when they are threatened. Almost all coloured frogs in the wild are poisonous.

Poison dart frogs

These are a group of beautifully coloured little frogs found in the humid areas of Central and South America. Most of their toxicity comes from a kind of ants they eat. Their skin secretes a deadly poison that can harm their predators. Hunters used to rub their arrows with these frogs' skin to collect poison on their arrows. This is how these frogs got their name. The blue poison dart frog, the golden poison frog and the strawberry poison dart frog are some of the most strikingly coloured frogs.

Facts

- Some frogs, like the Malaysian leapfrog, are brightly coloured to seem poisonous to predators.
- The Sonoran Desert toad secretes a poison that is known to have psychoactive properties.

Cane toads

Cane toads are big terrestrial toads found in Central and South America. They have an unusual capability of eating both living and dead creatures. They have large parotid glands that secrete a milky white fluid. Swallowing its tadpole can be very toxic for animals. It is used in many regions to kill insects that infest sugarcane plantations.

Fire-bellied toads

These toads from East Asia have a bright red-coloured underbelly that helps distract the predators. They arch on their back to display their strikingly contrasting colours. When attacked, their skin oozes a stinging, bad-tasting liquid, which repels predators.

> Name the toad that is used to kill insects in sugarcane plantations.

The World of Toads

Toads are tailless amphibians that are somewhat different from frogs. Toads have stubby bodies and shorter hind legs, which make them hop weakly. While frogs have a smooth and slimy skin, toads' skin is rough, dry and warty. Frogs are usually found in wetlands, whereas toads prefer dry lands.

Features

Most toads live on land but return to water to lay eggs. Their eggs look like strings of black beads held together by clear jelly. More than 300 kinds of toads are found all over the world. Toads are usually brown coloured and eat mosquitoes and insects. They mostly hibernate during the winter by burying themselves in the ground or under a rock. Most toads have a poison gland behind their eyes.

Eastern spadefoot toads

The Eastern spadefoot toad, from Massachusetts, has a long, sharp, sickle-shaped ridge on each of its hind legs, which gives it its name. Usually brown, black or olive in colour, they use their hind legs for burrowing. They are nocturnal toads and usually stay in shallow burrows.

Asian horned toads

The Asian horned toad is an interesting species of toad that looks like it has horns over its eyes. This toad has folds of patchy brown skin, which camouflages it wonderfully among dried leaves. It also has a large head with a fleshy snout.

Toads have a smooth and slimy skin. True/False?

Facts

- Toads help humans by killing plenty of insects.
- Natterjack toads are very noisy toads, and their calls can be heard across several kilometers.

Salamanders and Newts

Salamanders are a group of tailed amphibians. They resemble lizards and have long bodies and tails, short noses, four legs and moist skin. Most salamanders have four toes on their front feet and five toes on their rear feet. They do not have any claws or scales on their smooth bodies. They are secretive and voiceless nocturnal animals.

Sensing surroundings

Salamanders lack an external ear opening or eardrum. So, they have a poor sense of hearing. However, they have a very good eyesight, except for those that live in dark places. They also have the ability to pick up vibrations in water through their legs. Salamanders use their long tails as oars while swimming.

Habitat

Salamanders and newts are found only in the Americas and in the temperate zones of North Africa, Asia and Europe. Some salamander species are fully aquatic throughout their life, some are semi-aquatic and some are entirely terrestrial as adults. Terrestrial salamanders are mainly found in cool and shady places, such as under rocks or in damp burrows.

Mating

During the mating process, salamanders dance by waving their tails in front of their mates. When the dance is over, the male goes to the bottom of the water to deposit tiny cone-shaped spermatophores. The female moves over these sperms and collects them in her body so that her eggs can grow. The eggs hatch 30 days after they are laid. The tadpoles are ready to hunt as soon as they are born. They retain their tails all through their lives.

Facts

- Some arboreal salamanders use their tails for hanging or grasping.
- As salamanders grow, they lose the outer layer of their old skin and eat it.

Regeneration

Salamanders have the unique ability to regenerate lost limbs and body parts. This amazing adaptation is called autotomy. Whenever a salamander senses danger, it detaches its tail from the body. Some salamanders can grow tails, legs, organs and eyes, which might be of a colour different from the rest of the body.

What is the ability of salamanders to regenerate lost body parts called?

Unique Salamanders

There are around 350 species of salamanders. Many salamanders have bodies or characteristics different from standard or normal salamanders. Newts, mudpuppies, hellbenders and sirens all belong to the salamander family.

Newts

Newt is a common name for smaller salamanders. A newt is a salamander but a salamander may not be a newt. Newts have flattened tails that help them swim. They mainly stay on land from late summer to winter, returning to water only to breed during the spring.

Hellbenders

Hellbenders are large aquatic salamanders found in North America. They have thick bodies and broad and flat heads. These nocturnal amphibians mainly feed on fish.

Sirens

Sirens are salamanders that have lungs and gills at the same time. They have tiny lidless eyes and small front legs. They live in marshes and streams. They look like eels with no hind legs.

Facts

- A male newt stands on its hind and forelegs using its tail and does acrobatics for a female newt.
- The tiny pygmy salamander reaches up to a length of 5 cm and is one of the smallest salamanders in the world.

Mudpuppies

Mudpuppies or water dogs are aquatic salamanders that live in shallow lakes and streams. They have chunky bodies with four toes on each foot. Mudpuppies do not lose their gills after maturing into adults. They lack eyelids and the upper jaws.

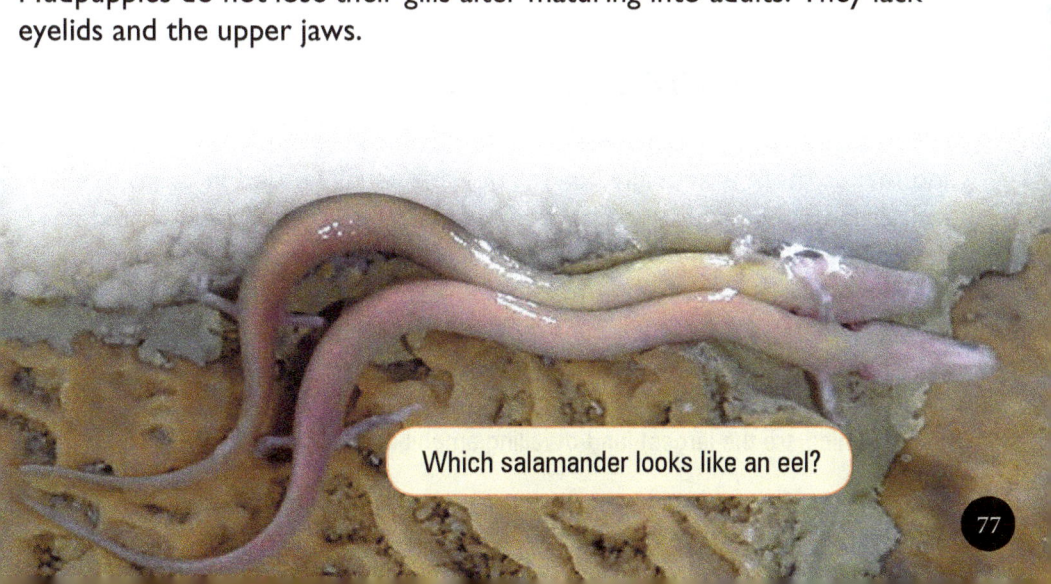

Which salamander looks like an eel?

Super Salamanders

Most salamanders are terrestrial as adults but some are aquatic. Salamanders are sometimes burrowing cave dwellers or arboreal. They usually live near water or in moist environments. Most salamanders are brightly coloured, particularly males during the breeding season.

Tiger salamanders

Tiger salamanders are long-tailed amphibians that are the largest land-dwelling salamanders on Earth. These salamanders have dark bodies that are marked with brilliant stripes or blotches. They are found in North America in dry plains, wet meadows and mountain forests.

North American blind salamanders

These salamanders have a whitish translucent skin that covers their eyes and makes them practically blind. They are usually found in caves, wells and streams. Olms are a type of blind salamander that have adapted to their underground life of complete darkness. These salamanders also lack any pigmentation and are whitish or pinkish in colour due to the lack of exposure to the sun.

> Which are the largest land-dwelling amphibians?

Facts

- The largest salamander in the world is the Chinese Giant Salamander. It can grow to a length of 5 feet.
- The Americans are home to more species of salamander than the rest of the world combined.

Giant salamanders

The rocky mountain streams and lakes in China are home to the largest amphibian species known as the Chinese giant salamander. It can reach up to a length of 1.8 m from head to tail and weigh up to 40 kg. These salamanders have a large head, wrinkly skin and poor vision. They are mainly aquatic, and their tail is usually half the length of their body.

Spotted salamanders

Spotted salamanders are bluish-black salamanders that are distinctly marked with bright yellow or orange spots. Spotted salamanders are often sold as pets and can live for as long as 20 to 30 years. These salamanders are mainly burrowing animals and often hibernate during winter.

Caecilians

Caecilians are a limbless and tailless tropical species of amphibians. Smaller caecilians resemble Earthworms and the larger ones resemble snakes. They are land dwellers and usually stay buried in the ground. This makes them the least-known group of amphibians.

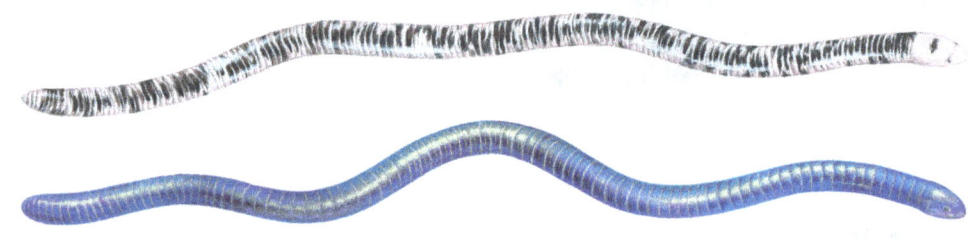

Appearance

Caecilians look like eels or worms but are not one of them. They have characteristics of vertebrates such as jaws and teeth. They have dozens of needle-sharp teeth in their mouth that are used to grab their prey. Their eyes are covered with skin or bones of the skull, making them virtually blind. A small sensory tentacle is present in front of the eye, which helps them to gather information. Most of them are between 12–35 cm long, but some can even get as long as 104 cm.

Typhlonectes

Caecilians come in some strikingly coloured varieties, including orange and grey with yellow stripes. A type of caecilian known as typhlonectes is commonly kept in aquariums pet. Typhlonectes is a fully aquatic caecilian found only in South America. It likes to burrow through the gravel and goes up for air several times a day.

Facts

- Caecilians can bury themselves in the ground in just a matter of two minutes.
- The three common groups of caecilians include beaked caecilians, fish caecilians and common caecilians.

Habitat

Caecilians are found primarily in the wet tropical regions of South America, South-East Asia and Central America. Since even terrestrial caecilians require a moist climate, they are normally found in swampy places in the tropical parts of the world. Many caecilians live their entire life hidden in burrows.

Typhlonectes is a type of _____ that can be kept as an aquarium pet.

Skin

The shiny skin of caecilians has many ring-shaped folds. Some species have scales under their skin. Their skin has glands that secrete toxins to escape predators.

Axolotls

Axolotls are a species of salamanders that do not grow beyond their larval stage. They do not develop lungs, protruding eyelids and other characteristics of adult salamanders. Axolotls have an unusual appearance and are found in vivid colours, including white, blue and grey. Commonly referred to as the Mexican walking fish, they are found in Lake Xochimilco and Lake Chalco in Mexico.

Breathing

One of the most unusual aspects of the axolotl is that it does not metamorphose into an adult. Unlike most amphibians that grow from water animals to land-dwelling amphibians, axolotls spend their entire lives in water. These salamanders retain their gills as they grow up. They have three pairs of external gills that protrude from the back of their head. They often come to the water surface for air.

Axolotls are also known as _____.

Breeding

Axolotls grow big enough to be able to breed with other species such as tiger salamanders. This amazing ability of axolotls is known as neoteny. Scientists believe that neoteny is a backward step in evolution. Axolotls reach their sexual maturity in approximately 12 months but are still in their larval stage. They are fairly hardy creatures that can live up to 15 years under proper conditions. Axolotls feed on snails, worms, small fish, and amphibians.

Facts

- Axolotls have amazing regenerative and healing capabilities.
- Most salamander larvae are much like axolotls before developing into adults.

Terrestrial axolotls

Axolotls have the ability to develop into land-dwelling adults if they are forced to leave their watery habitat and live on land for extended periods. The instances under which such changes take place are rare. They are critically endangered for several reasons, including pollution and the introduction of non-native fish into their habitat.

Endangered Amphibians

The global population of amphibians has been declining at an alarming rate since the 1980s. Nearly one-third of all amphibian species are threatened. Scientists have also reported serious malformations found in amphibians, including extra limbs and abnormal sex organs. There are various reasons for the dwindling populations of amphibians, many of which are a result of human activity.

Loss of habitat

Droughts are considered to be a major reason for the decline of amphibian population. Since amphibians lay their eggs in water, a lack of freshwater sites may be a possible cause. Destruction and transformation of wetlands to construct roads and agricultural sites is another major cause of the loss of their habitat.

Facts

- Up to 200 amphibian species have completely disappeared in the past 30 years.
- Some amphibians, such as the Puerto Rican crested toads have been saved from extinction by breeding lots of them in captivity.

Predators and food shortage

The shortage of food and an increasing number of predators also pose a threat to the amphibian population. Alien predators introduced in aquacultural basins, streams and other amphibian environments prey on amphibian eggs and larvae. Bullfrogs, which were introduced in western North America, are also believed to cause the decline of native amphibians by preying on them or competing with them for food.

Diseases

Many amphibians are known to have been affected by a fungus known as *Saprolegnia*. In 1997 researchers reported that the fungus was killing frogs in Panama's forest reserve, and frogs in Australia were found to be dying from a similar cause. Parasitic organisms are believed to cause deformities in amphibians.

Pesticides and ultraviolet radiation

According to research, amphibians at higher altitudes face extinction because of the harmful effects of ultraviolet radiation. Ultraviolet radiation was found to be killing the embryos of the long-toed salamander in the lakes of the Cascade Mountains. Pollution of water bodies by pesticides is also known to decrease the immunity of many amphibians.

What is Saprolegnia?

▲ *The California tiger salamander*

Glossary

Accumulate: to gather together

Arboreal: tree-dwelling

Climate: the type of weather a particular region has over a long period

Crustacean: a sea creature with several pairs of legs and a hard shell for protection

Endangered species: the species of animals that are at the risk of dying out

Extinct: having no living members

Fertilization: the process that begins the reproduction cycle in living beings

Fossil: decayed remains of ancient plants and animals buried deep inside the earth since millions of years

Fungus: a parasitic and spore-producing organism, such as yeast

Gastric juice: stomach juice that helps in the digestion of food

Glycogen: a form of glucose or sugar that provides energy

Habitat: a place where a particular animal lives

Hallucination: to imagine things, especially because of illness

Hibernation: a state of deep sleep in which an animal uses its accumulated fat to survive extreme weather conditions

Immunity: the ability of a living being to fight off germs, infections and diseases

Larynx: an organ in the throat that is responsible for producing sounds

Malformation: a part of the body that is formed abnormally

Marsupial: an animal that carries it baby in a pouch attached to its body

Nocturnal: active at night

Parasitic organism: an organism that lives on other animals for food and nutrition

Pesticide: a chemical that is used to kill creatures or pests that harm the growth of plants or crops

Pigmentation: the natural colour of skin

Predator: an animal that feeds on other animals

Prey: an animal that is eaten by predators

Psychoactive: something that affects an organism's mental state and behaviour

Rainforest: a forest in the tropical region, where it rains a lot

Startle: to surprise or amaze

Terrestrial: related to land

Tetrapod: a vertebrate animal having four limbs

Threatened species: those animal species that are on the verge of becoming endangered due to severe environmental changes and habitat loss

Ultraviolet light: a type of sunlight that is invisible to the naked human eye and is responsible for causing suntan and sunburns

Vertebrate: an animal with a backbone

Wetland: a land near a lake, river or any other water body that is partially covered with water

Answers

Page No. 50 False

Page No. 52 360 million

Page No. 55 Frogs and toads

Page No. 56 Alaska and above the Arctic Circle

Page No. 58 Gills

Page No. 61 Insects, worms and slugs

Page No. 63 Leopard frog

Page No. 65 Goliath frog

Page No. 66 7–9 days

Page No. 69 About 3500

Page No. 71 Cane toad

Page No. 73 False

Page No. 75 Autotomy

Page No. 77 Sirens

Page No. 78 Tiger salamanders

Page No. 81 Caecilian

Page No. 82 Mexican walking fish

Page No. 85 A fungus that affects amphibinans

www.ingramcontent.com/pod-product-compliance
Lightning Source LLC
Chambersburg PA
CBHW050657160426
43194CB00010B/1983